The Battle of the Coral Sea: The History and Legacy of World War II's First Major Battle Between Aircraft Carriers

By Charles River Editors

Picture of the explosion of the USS *Lexington* after the battle

About Charles River Editors

Charles River Editors provides superior editing and original writing services across the digital publishing industry, with the expertise to create digital content for publishers across a vast range of subject matter. In addition to providing original digital content for third party publishers, we also republish civilization's greatest literary works, bringing them to new generations of readers via ebooks.

Sign up here to receive updates about free books as we publish them, and visit Our Kindle Author Page to browse today's free promotions and our most recently published Kindle titles.

Introduction

The USS *Yorktown* shortly before the battle

The Battle of the Coral Sea

The growing buzz of aircraft engines disturbed the Japanese military construction personnel hauling equipment ashore on the beige coral sand of Tulagi island at 8:20 AM on May 4th, 1942. Offshore, the large IJN (Imperial Japanese Navy) minelayer Okinoshima, flagship of Admiral Shima Kiyohide, lay at anchor, along with two destroyers, Kikuzuki and Yutsuki, and transport ships. Six Japanese Mitsubishi F1M2 floatplanes also rested on the gentle, deep blue swell, marking Tulagi's future as an IJN floatplane base.

The men on the beach, at inland construction sites, or aboard the Japanese ships, looked up towards the huge white cumulus clouds sailing on the ocean wind. Taken completely by surprise, the Japanese stood and stared as 13 sturdy-looking dive bombers dropped through the cumulus layer at 6,000 feet, plunging towards the IJN ships. As they streaked lower, the white star on a black disc insignia of American aircraft grew visible on the underside of each wing.

As the dive bombers roared low, drowning out the soft clacking of palm-fronds agitated by the steady sea breeze, the dark capsule shapes of 1,000-lb bombs broke away from their undersides and hurtled towards the anchored ships. Amid the sudden thunder of explosions, huge fountains of white foam gushed upward, sparkling in the tropical sunlight before collapsing back into the sea.

Only as the American Douglas SBD-3 Dauntless dive bombers began climbing out of their attack did the Japanese finally open fire with the four anti-aircraft guns set up on the Tulagi shore. As Lieutenant Commander William Burch, leader of Scouting Five from the carrier USS Yorktown, later reported, "We took them by surprise, and they didn't start shooting at us until we pulled out [...] We hopped back over Guadalcanal, and landed aboard. [...] Only one plane had been hit by anti-aircraft. Its sway braces on the bomb rack were damaged. A couple of the dive bombers were attacked by a fighter on floats, but they shot him down. It was the only enemy plane we saw. What's more, I didn't see a ship sink." (Ludlum, 2006, 70).

Burch's assessment proved correct, with zero bomb hits scored. The telescopic sights and even the canopies of the SBD-3s fogged as they dropped from the cold of their cruising altitude to the thick, warm, moist jungle air hovering above Tulagi, spoiling the pilots' aim. However, the Japanese ordeal had not finished. Lieutenant Commander Joseph Taylor's Torpedo Five, a formation of 12 obsolete Douglas TBD-1 Devastator torpedo bombers, attacked shortly after Burch's SBD-3s. The first six aimed their torpedoes poorly, causing the ordnance to run up on the beach to explode harmlessly. The next six, however, scored a hit on Kikuzuki ("Chrysanthemum Moon"), inflicting 12 KIA and 22 WIA, and forcing the crew to beach their destroyer to avoid sinking. Other hits wrecked two small minelayers (Wa #1 and Wa #2) and the larger minelayer Tama Maru, which sank in 225 feet of water.

The Japanese, attacked throughout the day, radioed this information to the IJN task forces operating in the area. The unmistakable US carrier aircraft meant an American aircraft carrier sailed nearby, surprising the Japanese, who had not expected any enemy "flattops" in the Coral Sea near Australia at that time. In fact, the airstrikes on Admiral Shima's Tulagi invasion force marked the start of the strategically important Battle of the Coral Sea.

While the Battle of the Coral Sea is not as well known as other battles across the Pacific, it set a precedent by pitting enemy aircraft carriers against each other, a battle in which the rival navies themselves never sighted each other or fired a gun at each other. Instead, the fighting was done with the carriers' aircraft, something that would become more common over time and would result in decisive actions at places like Midway just months later. Furthermore, while it was in a sense a tactical victory for the Japanese, it would end up helping blunt their aggressive push east in the Pacific, making it a crucial strategic victory for the Allies.

The Battle of the Coral Sea: The History and Legacy of World War II's First Major Battle Between Aircraft Carriers analyzes the historic battle and the strategic importance it had in the

Pacific. Along with pictures of important people, places, and events, you will learn about the Battle of the Coral Sea like never before.

The Battle of the Coral Sea: The History and Legacy of World War II's First Major Battle Between Aircraft Carriers

About Charles River Editors

Introduction

Chapter 1: The Strategic Background

Japan's Pacific War against the United States was a massive gamble from the outset. When her seemingly endless struggle for the dominance of China had turned into an attritional slugging match, Japan had found it difficult to secure the raw materials she needed in order to continue, particularly rubber and oil. Lacking domestic supply, it might have been reasonable for Japan to plan on the basis of imports from other countries in Asia, but such supplies were largely controlled by Western democracies opposed to her expansion. Britain ruled Malaya, where most of the rubber might be sourced; while a Free Dutch administration still controlled Indonesia, despite Holland having been overrun by Japan's German allies in 1940. Indonesia had oil and rubber, but exports to Japan had been suspended by the colonial government. The alternative choice for oil was the USA herself, but she too opposed Japan's brutal imperial expansion, banning oil exports in 1941.

As a result, Japan therefore reasoned that it should seize a "Southern Resource Area" to address this problem. Once Malaya, Indonesia and other Allied holdings in Eastern Asia were secured, Japan would be able to prosecute and complete the war in China. Once that was done, Japan would be able to exploit Chinese economic potential fully, which was the main strategic goal.

For their parts, British, French and Dutch forces in Asia were weak. The British had their hands full with the war in Europe and Africa, and even Australia and New Zealand had sent most of their armies west. Therefore, a plan to grab the Southern Resource Area seemed entirely practical in military terms. Japan's main concern was determining the reaction of the United States to their maneuvers. Despite President Roosevelt's closeness to the British cause, he governed a nation which remained deeply isolationist in sentiment, and he had fought an election campaign in 1940 with promises that American boys were "not going to be sent into any foreign war"[1]. There might have been a chance that a Japanese attack on the European colonies in Asia would not have provoked a declaration of war from the U.S., but the Japanese government did not see it that way. They were convinced that an attack on Britain in particular would also bring war with the Americans.

Thus was born the desperate plan to launch a surprise attack on the U.S. fleet at Pearl Harbor, and until the summer of 1942, that gamble seemed as though it might have paid off. The initial hope was that the crushing blow dealt to the Americans at Pearl Harbor in December 1941 would induce the U.S. to sue for peace, but that proved to be a completely misplaced belief. The United States began fully mobilizing almost overnight, thanks to the peacetime draft Roosevelt had implemented; that bill helped the country's armed forces swell by two million within months of Pearl Harbor. In 1942 alone, 6 million men headed off to North Africa, Great Britain and the Pacific Ocean, carrying weapons in one hand and pictures of pin-up models like Betty Grable in

---

[1] Burns p6.

the other. Pearl Harbor had given Roosevelt the mandate he needed to prosecute world war against all of the axis powers.

As for the U.S. Pacific Fleet, it had been badly battered at Pearl Harbor, having all 8 battleships there incapacitated in the space of 90 minutes. It seemed like a disaster, but was it? The USS *Pennsylvania* had been in dry dock anyway, and five of the others would also eventually return to service. Furthermore, the Pacific War which Japan had just started would end up proving that there was a new queen of the fleet: the aircraft carrier. America's untouched carrier squadron was already cutting through the ocean in pursuit, a mark of things to come. Furthermore, elaborate Japanese preparations to capitalize on the attack with their submarines came to nothing. Although they had strung a picket of 23 large fleet subs around the Hawaiian Islands to interdict any surface traffic after the battle, they had almost no success, because the Americans were able to shift several of their big units out of the harbor within days unmolested, and reinforcements moved in the other direction. Similarly, expectations for the five midget submarines the Japanese had launched on the eve of the attack had not been met, as all five were abandoned or destroyed (though it's now believed that one of them may have managed to slip into the harbor and fire her torpedoes).

For a time, Japanese strategists could contemplate a contingency plan even if the U.S. proved ready to fight. If they couldn't knock America out with one opening blow, perhaps they could sap her will to fight by presenting the Southern Resource Area as a fait accompli. This would be followed by a series of further blows against the U.S. Navy, designed to push her well behind in the race to catch up with Japan's naval strength. Having crippled the American fleet and secured her Resource Area, Japan could assert that she had no further imperial ambitions, and a chastened America might concede the point rather than face years of attritional warfare across the Pacific. It was another variation of the original plan, but again it relied on a misunderstanding of America's will to fight. Having failed to knock the USA out after Pearl Harbor, and in the light of America's ultimate ability to field far more units than Japan could ever dream of, it was all she had.

For those thinking along these lines, the opening months of the Pacific War provided some solace. Japan's thinly spread but highly effective forces swept south and west, securing those areas she deemed to be vital to her future. The tiny British garrison in Hong Kong was easily snuffed out, and far more importantly, Japan sank two British battleships off Malaya, landed an army there and moved down the peninsula. In doing so she subdued independent Thailand almost en passant. In Britain's worst ever military defeat, her army of 130,000 surrendered at Singapore in February 1942. Japan also moved into Burma and within four months was threatening the border with British India. At the same time, the Philippines was attacked, with most of America's Far Eastern Airforce destroyed on the ground during the first few hours. Although MacArthur's besieged army would cling on to the Bataan peninsula until May, Manila and the rest of the country were secured by the end of January 1942.

Meanwhile, Japanese invasion forces had also conquered the Dutch East Indies, thereby securing an enclave on the northern coast of New Guinea which threatened to expose the defence of Australia. Indeed, in February, Japanese aircraft bombed Darwin. Japan also grabbed the Solomon Islands, a British protectorate screening the northeast coast of Australia. To complete the picture, the American holdings of Wake and Guam fell, leaving the island of Midway as the most westerly American base in the central Pacific. Even French Indo-China was effectively in Japanese hands, because the Vichy government had acquiesced to Japanese military occupation in December 1941.

A glance at the map in April 1942 would therefore show a huge expanse of the Pacific region now controlled by Japan. In less than four months, Japan had humiliated American and Allied forces, and her land acquisitions were matched by naval success. The attack on Pearl Harbor had neutralized most of the battleships in the U.S. Pacific Fleet, and in addition to the loss of the battleships *Prince of Wales* and *Repulse* off Malaya, the British lost the aircraft carrier *Hermes* to Japanese aircraft in April when they raided deep into the Indian Ocean. This caused the British to pull their Pacific Fleet right back to Mombasa in East Africa. The Americans, Dutch and Australians had lost further vessels as well, notably at the battle of the Java Sea in February.

As a result, when the summer of 1942 started, the only significant naval threat remaining to Japan in the Pacific was what remained of the American Pacific Fleet following the attack on Pearl Harbor, and some of those battleships had been pulled back to San Francisco. This fact was not known by Japan, but given their superiority in battleships, the Japanese were not overly concerned about the remnants of the American fleet either way. What had remained untouched by the attack on Pearl Harbor were the American carriers; if these could be destroyed, then Japan would have secured all of her objectives. At that stage, perhaps, there might be a further opportunity to press the Allies for some kind of peace treaty, cementing Japan's new empire into place.

The Japanese flagship carrier *Akagi* in April 1942

In May however, things would begin to turn around.

Chapter 2: Operation Mo

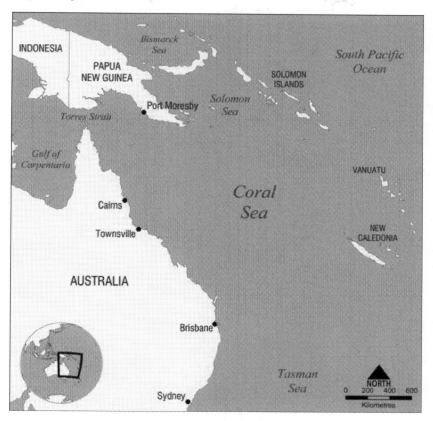

Norman Einstein's map of the Coral Sea

The Battle of the Coral Sea resulted from an IJN operation codenamed Operation Mo, aimed at simultaneously taking Port Moresby on the southeast coast of New Guinea and bombing the important airfields at Charters Towers and Townsville in northeast Australia. The Japanese high command hoped to cut off Australia's lines of communication with the United States through this operation.

The Japanese abandoned the notion of invading Australia as impractical at the start of 1942, but they still hoped to isolate the Commonwealth nation, and if the Japanese acquired Port

Moresby, they could also loose land-based bombers against military targets and cities in Australia. By these methods, Prime Minister Tojo Hideki hoped to force Australia out of the war. The ethnically English nation "Down Under" provided hard-fighting soldiers to the Allies and excellent submarine bases to the Americans.

Tojo

Typically for the IJN, the Japanese prepared an excessively intricate plan for Operation Mo. The Japanese chose Port Moresby as the main target in part because of numerous night bombing raids launched from there against important IJN facilities at Rabaul, and in part because it enabled attacks on Australia proper. At the same time, the Japanese scheme relied on perfect coordination between five completely separate forces to succeed. The South Seas Force plan called for the "Tulagi Invasion Force" to leave Rabaul on April 29th. The Moresby Escort Fleet left Truk on April 29th also, while the Moresby Main Force would leave Truk on April 30th. The Moresby Carrier Force would depart Truk on May 1st, and the Moresby Invasion Force sortie from Rabaul on May 4th. The 25th Air Flotilla provided air support.

Among the unit movement orders issued by Combined Fleet HQ, the Carrier Force received Secret South Seas Fleet Operational Order Number 13, which described the maneuvers to be used (and used the designation "x" for the day of the projected landings at Port Moresby) and read in part:

"Sortie from Truk towards the Solomon Islands on about day x–10 through waters to the north-east, and then continue to provide direct support for the Tulagi invasion operation. On day x–5 (the day after the start of reconnaissance flying boat patrols from Tulagi) enter the Coral Sea from the east of the Solomon Islands, begin to provide direct support to the Moresby Invasion Force as required, according to the following strategies.

"a. When a powerful naval force is detected, first attack and destroy[...]

"c. Up until day x+5 after the successful landing at Port Moresby, continue preparations for the appearance of a powerful enemy naval force in the area of the Coral Sea within range of Japanese airbases." (Bullard, 2007, 58).

The orders went on to state that while strong American naval forces probably would not be present, the English Royal Navy might scrape together a force of destroyers and a few light and heavy cruisers to harass the Port Moresby landings. The route given for the Japanese carriers caused them to enter the Coral Sea from the east, between San Cristobal (now Makira) in the Solomon Islands and Espiritu Santo in the New Hebrides archipelago.

The Japanese aimed for surprise with this route, rather than entering the Coral Sea from the north as the Allies probably expected. The Japanese carriers would screen the invasion force while steaming towards Australia, launching a surprise attack against Townsville and Charters Towers airfields. Since these airfields lay well beyond Japanese land-based aircraft range from the nearest Imperial airfields, their aircraft complements – the Japanese hoped – would prove vulnerable to a sudden, massive carrier strike.

Vice Admiral Inoue Shigeyoshi held overall command over the South Seas Force (Japanese 4th Fleet), remaining at Rabaul to attempt coordination of the armada's numerous branches. Meanwhile, Rear Admiral Takagi Takeo held command over the Moresby Carrier Force. Eventually killed in action at the Battle of Saipan in 1944, Rear Admiral Takagi led a force centered around the two major fleet carriers *Shokaku* and *Zuikaku* in the Coral Sea. Vessels of the *Shokaku* class represented the finest aircraft carriers in the Pacific until the 1943 advent of the superior USN *Essex*-class. However, since Takagi lacked any background in carrier warfare, he commanded the escorting cruisers and destroyers, delegating full control over the *Shokaku* and *Zuikaku* to Rear Admiral Hara Chuichi. Hara, an exceptionally tall, beefy man by the standards of the short, slender Japanese of the mid-20th century, received the nickname "King Kong," both for his large physique and for his hard-charging energy.

Inoue

Takeo

Hara

Optimism characterized the Japanese mood at all levels as the Port Moresby expedition sailed in late April and early May. As the official Japanese military records state, the officers and men showed themselves "in high spirits for adventure." (Bullard, 2007, 61). The Americans, meanwhile, set about preparing to offer them more adventure than they bargained for.

Operation Mo relied heavily on the element of surprise to achieve its objectives, and the Japanese failed to realize they had lost that crucial element thanks to the skilled U.S. Navy code-breakers, and the prickly, independent-minded, outspoken young captain Joseph Rochefort in particular. Rochefort managed to tease a workable outline of the Operation Mo plans out of fragmentary, cryptic intercepts of Japanese signals and orders. This knack ensured his position as one of the chief Pacific code-breakers despite his tendency to speak his mind forcefully to high-ranking officers. Another code-breaker, Thomas Dyer, explained Rochefort's singular skill and the crucial effect it had on the Pacific war, noting that it "was his ability – to make a silk purse out of a sow's ear. [...] The early messages about Coral Sea were perfectly capable of being read in a totally different way than the correct way. Knowledge of the character of the Japanese and this, that, and the other, enabled him to get the right meaning." (Carson, 2011, 269).

Rochefort

Rochefort correctly identified a mystifying codename, RZP, as referring to Port Moresby, though Admiral Chester Nimitz still doubted if this represented the actual Japanese objective. More certainly the voluminous radio chatter pointed to a massive buildup at Rabaul and Truk. On April 17th, Rochefort and the other code-breakers finally convinced Nimitz, a vigorous and effective leader who became one of America's small constellation of five-star admirals, that the Japanese thunderhead gathering at Rabaul would sweep south, not east. Nimitz signaled his intention to move forces into the Coral Sea to his superior Admiral Ernest J. King, C-in-C US Fleet.

The fierce, secretive, energetic King, whom President Franklin D. Roosevelt quipped probably "shaved with a blowtorch" (Toll, 2012, 166), concurred with Nimitz's (and Rochefort's) analysis, guessing quite closely when the Japanese planned to launch the invasion. He also backed Nimitz's decision to send carriers into the Coral Sea.

Thus, to counter the Japanese threat, Nimitz dispatched two task forces into the ocean bounded by Australia, Papua New Guinea, and the Solomon Islands. American doctrine still used one aircraft carrier as the core of a separate task force at this point in the war (the Coral Sea engagement would permanently change that idea), but Nimitz combined two such task forces. He ordered Task Force 17, based on *USS Yorktown* with Rear Admiral Frank "Jack" Fletcher commanding, and Task Force 11, centered on *USS Lexington,* under Rear Admiral Aubrey "Jake" Fitch, to rendezvous quickly and counter the Japanese threat. Frank Fletcher received overall command.

Nimitz

Fletcher

Nimitz sent the following orders to Fletcher: "An enemy offensive in New Guinea dash Solomon area is at present indicated for first week of May probable primary objective Moresby. May eventually include three or four carriers [and] about 80 heavy bombers and same number of fighters at New Guinea and New Britain air bases. Your task [is to] assist checking further advance by enemy in above area by seizing favorable opportunities to destroy ships, shipping, and aircraft." (Lundstrom, 2006, 132).

These orders strongly resembled those usually issued by the German Wehrmacht but far less common in other military establishments of the era. The German army provided an objective but left the method of achieving it entirely to the initiative of the commander on the scene, which, given the high professionalism of the Wehrmacht, often produced excellent results. Nimitz followed the same procedure with Fletcher, allowing the admiral leeway in how to achieve his objectives, though in this case with a mixed outcome.

The two American carriers and their escorting destroyers and cruisers met at the rendezvous coordinates codenamed Point Buttercup at dawn on May 1st. On the same day, the Japanese carriers sailed from Truk in accordance with the timetable laid down in Secret Order Number 13. The USS *Chicago* and *Perkins* also joined the USN task force, while two Australian cruisers – the light HMAS *Hobart* and the heavy *HMAS Australia* under Rear Admiral John Gregory Crace - would join the flotilla southwest from Guadalcanal on May 4th.

Crace

Fletcher wanted his ships ready for whatever action ensued, and so commenced fueling from oilers such as the USS *Neosho* as soon as the rendezvous occurred. The Rear Admiral desired full bunkers so that in the event of protracted maneuvering, lack of fuel would not force an American withdrawal or even leave one of his ships dead in the water. At this point, he expected refueling to conclude on May 5th, at which point his entire combined armada could move out in search of the foe. Ultimately, events did not cooperate with this leisurely schedule.

The Australians, by now well aware of the Japanese advance thanks to Allied signals intelligence, removed their civil personnel and garrison from Tulagi on May 1st. Lying between Malaita to the northeast and Guadalcanal to the south, Tulagi provided the site for the Solomon Islands protectorate's administrative center due to its relative freedom from malaria and other dangerous tropical diseases, rife on other islands of the chain.

On May 3rd, Admiral Shima's invasion force arrived at Tulagi, temporarily supported by the light aircraft carrier *Shoho*. The *Shoho* stood by, ready to launch aircraft to provide close air support to the invading troops in case the Australians mounted a determined defense. However, the troops wading ashore met with nothing more threatening than the sound of waves on the coral sand beach, palms stirring in the wind, and the voices of birds and insects. Accordingly, the *Shoho* sailed away to participate in other duties. Japanese engineers of the Eighth Base Unit and the Seventh Construction Section waded in through the surf, and, inside a cordon of soldiers, started to build the structures needed for a future floatplane base. Half a dozen Mitsubishi F1M2 "Pete" floatplanes arrived from Rabaul, their distinctive biplane design making them stand out among Japanese aircraft even without their seaplane fittings.

As a result, the Japanese of the Tulagi invasion force enjoyed a relaxed, upbeat mood, expecting another easy victory after six months of such triumphs.

Chapter 3: First Contact on May 4

Rear Admiral Fletcher, on board the *Yorktown,* received alarming news on May 2nd, with his planned refueling still underway. Nimitz sent a signal that the Japanese had sailed and likely begun their incursion into the Coral Sea, based on decoded radio intercepts analyzed by the indefatigable American code-breakers. Fletcher immediately split his force, placing it at considerable risk. While the *Lexington* continued to fuel, the *Yorktown* and 10 escorting cruisers and destroyers sailed out into the Coral Sea. There, he awaited further news so that he could move to intercept and attack Japanese fleet assets as soon as he learned their position.

While splitting his force represented an act of recklessness, this did not represent a personal failing on Fletcher's part. At this point in time, underdeveloped American naval doctrine called for aircraft carriers to operate individually. This doctrine would be gone within a month, swept away by the effectiveness of multiple carriers working together in the coming battle and at the Battle of Midway, but that still lay in the future.

The Australians naturally sent regular reconnaissance flights towards the Solomon Islands, watching for any signs of the expected invasion, and on the afternoon of May 3rd, Australian pilots spotted a force of Japanese ships bearing down rapidly on Tulagi. They passed the information to their superiors, who in turn transmitted it to the commander of the Allied aircraft carriers. Fletcher, loitering in the Coral Sea aboard the *Yorktown,* immediately ordered the aircraft carrier to sail north towards Tulagi after he received the Australian message at 7 PM on the 3rd. In a stroke of good fortune for the Americans, stormy weather closed in as a cold front advanced. Though the rain lashing down over the decks and the heavy swell made conditions uncomfortable for the crews above decks, they also concealed the isolated aircraft carrier from Japanese aircraft or submarines.

When day broke on May 4th, the *Yorktown* and its escorts lay 100 miles south of Guadalcanal, on the far side from Tulagi. A heavy overcast still prevailed, with strong winds and periodic rain squalls. Despite the rather unfavorable flying conditions, however, the men appeared eager for action, excited at the prospect of finally launching a counterstrike at the "Japs" who had enjoyed unbroken successes until then.

Fletcher sent no escorting fighters with the strike forces launched, instead keeping the fighters orbiting the *Yorktown* as a combat air patrol (CAP). The ship sent out three waves – Scouting Five, made up of 13 SBD-3 dive bombers under William Burch, Bombing Five, comprising 15 SBD-3s under Wallace Short, and Torpedo Five, 12 TBD-1 torpedo bombers under Joseph Taylor. The formations flew due north over Guadalcanal at 17,000 feet, passing through heavy rain squalls and gusty winds above the island's jungle-covered mountains. The meteorological conditions made flying difficult, but it also hid the Americans from Japanese scouting aircraft.

The American strike waves broke out into clear sunlight past Guadalcanal, with a cumulus cloud deck at 6,000 feet. At 8:20 AM, Burch's Bombing Five launched the first attack on the Japanese ships at Tulagi.

With steam already up, the Japanese vessels got underway immediately, abandoning the harbor in an effort to escape the American attacks, but this tactic only offered partial success. For hours, the American pilots hunted the Japanese ships, shuttling back and forth over Guadalcanal to rearm and refuel, then flying out to attack again. In the manner of the pilots of every nation, they claimed to have populated the ocean richly with Japanese cruisers, battleships, and other heavy warships, when in fact they only faced a pair of destroyers and a mix of light minelayers and transports. They also claimed they sank far more vessels than the handful the Japanese actually lost. David Berry, piloting a 1,000-lb bomb equipped SBD-3, described a successful attack on a Japanese "gunboat," which was actually a small minelayer, probably *Wa #1* or *Wa #2*: "Sam [Adams] dove and missed. […] I was next. I missed, too. […] When I pulled out, I looked back and saw a bomb hit. I think it was Rawley's. […] When the smoke and debris subsided, there were a few crates in the water – a big reddish-brown splotch – but no ship. Rawley's bomb blew that gunboat into a thousand pieces, and she just disappeared." (Ludlum, 2006, 72).

Admiral Shima himself experienced a close call during the repeated American attacks. An SBD-3 dove at his ship, the large minelayer *Okinoshima,* with murderous intent. However, the USN pilot dove straight into a cumulus cloud, which momentarily confused him. He released his 1,000-lb bomb slightly too soon, and it plunged into the water very close to the minelayer rather than punching through its deck. Nevertheless, the shock sufficed to scramble or damage machinery throughout the *Okinoshima*, and other ships later took Shima's flagship under tow for Truk to receive repairs.

The *Okinoshima*

The Japanese floatplanes took to the air to attack the less maneuverable SBD-3s. In response, Fletcher released a quartet of Grumman F4F Wildcat fighters. The rugged, high-speed Wildcats, living up to their name, tore the floatplanes to shreds, shooting down three to crash in the thick jungles of Guadalcanal. The F4F Wildcats then pounced on the second Japanese destroyer *Yuzuki*, riddling the vessel with .50 caliber machine gun bullets from stem to stern as it tried to escape. Nine crew and the captain, Hirota Tachibana, died in the hail of half-inch diameter slugs, and the ship soon trailed a long banner of leaking fuel oil over the sea surface as it limped towards distant Rabaul.

Lost in the clouds, one TBD Devastator torpedo bomber and two F4F Wildcats ran out of fuel, forcing their crews to land – the TBD ditching in the ocean, the F4Fs landing on the Guadalcanal beach. The two F4F pilots, Scott McCuskey and J.P. Adams, met a group of friendly natives, who showed them to a fresh stream and brought them coconuts to eat, while the two Americans rigged an improvised tent from a parachute. That evening, the destroyer USS *Hammann* managed a rescue of the men despite violent surf. Meanwhile, the destroyer USS *Perkins* searched for the crew of the TBD, including Lieutenant Leonard Emil Ewoldt, but could not find them. However, the Americans found and rescued Ewoldt later. The Lieutenant received the Navy Cross for his participation in the Tulagi attack and lived to the age of 87 years in Hartley, Iowa.

The attack on Tulagi by American carrier-based aircraft, clearly identified by sharp-eyed observers among the Japanese, surprised the IJN. This could only mean that, contrary to their previous faulty intelligence, at least one USN aircraft carrier, and probably more, had entered the Coral Sea. Borne high on a tide of victories up to this point, the Japanese Combined Fleet HQ issued a statement expressing their aggressive satisfaction with this turn of events: "Having confidence in the strength of the 5th Air Flotilla, it will be possible to catch and destroy the enemy aircraft carriers that have eluded us since the beginning of the war. In addition to bringing us great joy, this will inform the enemy appropriately of our strength. The South Seas Fleet has yearned for suitable hard fighting, given that there was a good chance of receiving raids from enemy carriers up until the completion of the Port Moresby operation." (Bullard, 2007, 61).

The Americans aboard *Yorktown,* including Fletcher, celebrated what they believed represented a great victory. Prudently, however, Fletcher retreated south during the early hours of May 5th, slipping away into the storms and squalls along the cold front. Now that they had been suddenly alerted to the presence of at least one American carrier in the Coral Sea, the Moresby Carrier Force started hunting for the USN ships. The Japanese, eager for battle, remained confident that they would soon send their enemies to a grave in the black, crushing depths a mile and a half under the Coral Sea's rolling swell.

Chapter 4: Searching for the Enemy, May 5-6

On the morning of May 5th, the triumphant *Yorktown* and its escorts emerged from beneath the cold front clouds into brilliant sunlight sparkling on the wave crests of the dark ocean, and a bit later, the ships of Task Force 17 rejoined *Lexington* and Task Force 11. Rear Admiral Aubrey Fitch flew over to the *Yorktown* to talk with Fletcher, finding the carrier's crew in an exultant mood after their success at Tulagi, greatly inflated by the pilots' description of the ships they sank as light and heavy cruisers.

Fletcher, believing himself safe for the moment, sent out numerous scouting aircraft missions. He also ordered the ships to continue refueling from the fast oiler *Neosho*. Fletcher's emphasis on frequent refueling proved wise, as it helped greatly to maintain the overall mobility of his ships, and the *Neosho* would soon suffer ruinous damage at the hands of Japanese pilots, further confirming Fletcher's choice in fueling when able.

The Australian vessels of Task Force 44 commanded by Rear Admiral John Crace joined the other two task forces at the rendezvous area designated Point Corn. Lieutenant Commander Paul Stroop, a staff officer aboard the *Lexington,* later recalled Crace's opinions about the shared mission: "I remember quite distinctly the first communication that we had from our Royal Navy friend, Admiral Crace, had to do with his evaluation of the importance of the Coral Sea area. [...] he said that he considered this area of the greatest importance and our combined forces should do everything they could to keep the Japanese from coming in to the Coral Sea area." (Wooldridge, 1993, 37).

In the meantime, the Moresby Carrier Force under Admiral Takagi approached the vicinity of Tulagi, sending aircraft and ships to investigate the situation. Like Fletcher, Takagi had focused on refueling his carriers and their escorts for prolonged maneuvering on the Coral Sea, but ordered the refueling operation broken off when heard of the American attack at Tulagi, hoping to catch a carrier unawares.

The Carrier Force discovered Admiral Shima had aborted the operation after losing both his destroyers and various minelayers, plus most of the six F1M2 floatplanes. The *Kikuzuki* lay on the beach, soon to slide off at high tide and sink in the coastal shallows. The USN later towed it to Purvis Bay, where its stripped, rusting hulk remains.

Shima had embarked all of the expedition's men and sent them to join the Port Moreby invasion force, judging the Tulagi venture too damaged and too exposed to the Americans to continue. The Port Moresby invasion force had left Rabaul and sailed south into the Coral Sea on May 5th. The light carrier *Shoho* rejoined this armada after having provided initial air cover to the Tulagi landing.

The Japanese sent out their Type 97 Kawanishi H6K flying boats, four-engine twin-tailed aircraft with a then-remarkable range of 4,112 miles, which made them capable of staying in the air for 24 hours at cruising speed. They also appeared quite large to carrier crews, accustomed to such craft as the F4F Wildcat, 28 feet long with a 38 foot wingspan; a Kawanishi measured 84 feet long with a 131 foot wingspan, carrying a crew of 9 men.

An H6K

Towards the evening of May 5th, one such Kawanishi approached the *Lexington* above a layer of stratus clouds, hidden from the ships below. However, Lieutenant Commander James Flatley, part of the *Yorktown's* F4F combat air patrol 12 miles from his home carrier, spotted the large

Japanese aircraft and moved to attack, as Stanley Johnston, aboard the *Lexington,* reported: "We could see neither Flatley nor the Jap, both being above the cloud level. At this point the *Lexington*'s fighter director Lieut. 'Red' Gill broke in to ask Flatley: 'Where is the Kawanishi?' 'Wait a minute, and I'll show him to you,' Flatley replied. [...] Then suddenly there was a glow in the clouds like a ball of fire. It increased and then there popped out of the vapor a huge plane, spinning madly and burning like a torch [...] It hit the water [...] and instantly exploded. There was a big flash of flame and then nothing but a huge pillar of black smoke." (Johnston, 1942, 158).

The Japanese crew either sent no radio message about the carriers prior to their deaths, or else they did so but failed to reach Admiral Takagi. Radio communications in the Coral Sea proved problematic for both sides at around this time, possibly due in part to the unsettled weather. Nevertheless, the canny Japanese noted the Kawanishi's failure to return and correctly guessed that the American carriers could be found in the patrol area assigned to that particular aircraft.

On the night of May 5th and the early morning hours of the 6th, Fletcher sailed his armada south, refueling while in motion from the fast oilers built for precisely this purpose, such as the *Neosho*. The men on the *Neosho* carried out their duties with great professionalism, though the oiler suffered battering by large waves and some of its crew endured injuries when massive seas poured over its decks. Photographs from the Coral Sea show men clinging desperately to the rails while much of the ship's structure around them is hidden in masses of raging foam.

The *Neosho*

Admiral Takagi also turned his thoughts to topping off his detachment's oil bunkers once it became clear that the Americans did not choose to lurk near Tulagi. The Moresby Carrier Force sailed west into the Coral Sea, meeting a Japanese fleet oiler 180 miles westward from Guadalcanal on the morning of May 6th.

The American code-breakers continued to monitor and interpret Japanese signals traffic. On the night of May 5th to 6th, they intercepted a fragmentary radio signal they believed had ordered Takagi's carrier to move towards Australia and launch airstrikes against the airfields there. In this case, the usually reliable Joseph Rochefort, star of the *Hypo* decoding unit, botched his job badly. Inoue, in fact, had ordered Takagi to ignore Australia, giving him a seek-and-destroy mission against the American carrier group.

Based on this faulty data, Fletcher reversed course during the night, heading back northwest to find the Japanese carriers. In the meantime, more flying boats reported the approximate American position. On the afternoon of May 6th, Takagi sailed south with those ships that had refueled in search of the Americans. The hostile forces now moved forward on a near-collision course, with neither certain of the other's location.

Admiral Fitch summarized the American analysis of the situation on the 6th: "Naval units, including one carrier and the invasion fleet were reported converging on Deboyne Island. It was expected that the enemy would use Jomard Entrance to enter the Coral Sea. Two more CVs, probably Carrier Division Five, were reported in the vicinity of Bougainville Island, on May 6 [...] Carrier Division Five [was expected to] run southward from the vicinity of Bougainville and might be within striking distance on the morning of May 7." (Lundstrom, 2006, 157).

This statement shows how deeply the fog of war had hidden the Japanese location from Fletcher and his crews. Fitch placed the Japanese carriers 500 miles distant, but at the moment when he made this analysis, their actual location lay just 170 miles away and closing.

Luckily for Fletcher and the American Task Force as a whole, the Japanese received equally faulty information in the afternoon. A Kawanishi crew mistakenly reported the American forces as sailing south at the time they were actually heading northwest. Thus, Rear Admiral Hara "King Kong" Chuichi took the carriers south in pursuit.

On the night of May 6th and the early morning hours of the 7th, Fletcher's Task Force 17 (the umbrella designation for the combined forces of the original Task Forces 17, 11, and 44) and Hara's carriers passed within 70 miles of one another without realizing the proximity of their enemies. The Japanese moved past on the east, chasing Fletcher south, while Fletcher sailed by on the west chasing the Japanese north.

Fitch, aboard the *Yorktown,* ordered the SBDs armed with one 500-lb bomb and a pair of 100-lb bombs in place of the standard 1,000-lb bomb on the evening of the 6th. Fortunately for the SBD-3 Dauntless pilots, Commander Henry "Hap" Arnold, the ship's air officer, had already had his crews arm the SBDs with the larger, more effective ordnance. Not wishing to give away the position of his ship by sending the men out to change the bomb loads using flashlights for illumination, the beams of which might be seen for some distance over the dusk-wrapped ocean surface, Captain Elliot Buckmaster, the *Yorktown's* skipper, countermanded Fitch's order, and his decision stood.

One other important development occurred on May 6th. Fletcher formed a separate task unit, Task Force 17.3, under the Australian Rear Admiral John Crace, to speed ahead to the Louisiade Archipelago and dispute the Jomard Passage with the Port Moresby Invasion Force. Crace's command included three cruisers and three destroyers. Simultaneously, Fletcher detached the fast oiler *Neosho* and sent the doughty vessel south – towards safety, as he then believed. He detached the destroyer USS *Sims* to escort the valuable refueling ship, though the extra protection seemed almost superfluous.

Chapter 5: May 7

At dawn on May 7th, the Moresby Invasion Force, including the light carrier *Shoho,* moved into the Jomard Passage, the channel between Papua New Guinea on the north and the Louisiade Archipelago to the south, connecting the Solomon Sea and the Coral Sea. As the sun rose in a clear sky over the invasion force and *Shoho* moved into the vicinity of Misima Island, Captain Izawa Ishinosuke sent out scouts in a search pattern southward, looking for American aircraft carriers. 115 miles south of the Louisades, and sailing north under clear skies, Rear Admiral Crace's three cruisers and three destroyers kept a sharp lookout for the invasion force. Further south still, the mass of Fletcher's Task Force 17 sailed northwest, at a slower speed.

At daybreak, a cold front from the south dominated the weather at Fletcher's location. A thick layer of cumulus clouds covered the sky, with rain squalls trailing to the ocean surface at intervals. A cool wind blew in gusts, raising a choppy sea.

With visibility limited to around 10 miles, the Americans hoped to obtain cover from Japanese airstrikes. Since they still believed the Japanese carriers lay to their north, this would give them an advantage, as clear skies and unlimited visibility prevailed northward. Staff officer Lieutenant Commander Paul Stroop, aboard the *Lexington,* described the American actions as morning broke over the roughened surface of the Coral Sea: "The battle plan was quite standard. It was something that we had used in peacetime maneuvers. We simply drew a limiting circle in the direction of the area of interest and assigned planes to go out on radii so that at the outer end of their search they would be twice visual distance apart. In other words, the objective was to cover the outer limits of your search sector completely. This was visual search, using the scouting planes, which went out about 175 miles." (Wooldridge, 1993, 37).

The stout, cylindrical shapes of the SBD dive bomber scouts buzzed off the decks of both carriers and skimmed away under the gray and white canopy of densely packed cumulus clouds, buffeted by wind gusts. Meanwhile, 200 miles east, the Japanese fleet carriers launched their own scouting aircraft, many directed southward, where Takagi believed the American carrier force might be found. On the decks of both American and Japanese carriers, dive bombers, fighters, and torpedo bombers idled, their engines rumbling and propellers turning slowly, awaiting news of potential targets.

The actions of the American and Japanese forces – and their mistakes – continued to mirror one another eerily. At 8:15 AM, Lieutenant John Nielsen flew north of Misima Island and spotted two cruisers and two destroyers of the Port Moresby Invasion Force. He signaled this fact to Task Force 17 and turned for home. However, the signaling device used included a mechanical fault unknown to Nielson. This switched the codes for ship types one position, so that the signal he sent actually reported two aircraft carriers and two cruisers. Fletcher, receiving this signal, believed Nielsen had located Takagi's 5th Carrier Division, moving in advance of the Moresby Invasion Force – a not unreasonable assumption. Thus, the Americans sailed north to close the distance and bring the two putative targets within range of their carrier craft.

At 9:15 AM, Fitch judged the contact now close enough and loosed the full aerial might of Task Force 17 against the reported carriers. This force consisted of 53 SBD-3 Dauntless dive bombers, 22 TBD-1 Devastator torpedo bombers, and 8 F4F fighters. The Americans were unwittingly launching their attack waves against non-carrier ships, believing they had found the Japanese fleet carriers.

Far to the south, events in the Japanese task force roughly mirrored the Americans' erroneous actions. A Japanese floatplane spotted the fast oiler *Neosho* and the escorting destroyer *Sims* at 7:22 AM, radioing excitedly that an American aircraft carrier and a cruiser lay 163 miles south of 5th Carrier Division's position. Takagi hesitated to act on a single report, but at 7:45 AM, another floatplane crew made the same mistake.

Now convinced that the *Neosho* was the *USS Saratoga,* Takagi and Hara unleashed a massive 78-plane attack against the American vessels to the south. Beginning around 8:30 AM, the attack consisted of 36 Aichi D3A2 dive bombers (relatively slow aircraft at 267 mph, carrying a single 551-lb bomb), 24 Nakajima B5N2 "Kate" torpedo bombers (capable of being equipped with a single 1,760-lb Type 91 torpedo, one 1,760-lb bomb, two 551-lb bombs, or six 293-lb bombs as payload), and 18 agile, long-range Mitsubishi A6M "Zero" fighters.

A short time later, as the American strike flew north and the Japanese strike flew south, both against incorrectly identified targets, each commander abruptly received new information apprising him of his error. However, each commander, for his own reasons, proved reluctant to recall his strike force, which led to very different outcomes for the two sides.

Nielsen, returning from his scouting mission, dropped a message on the deck "confirming" the sighting of four light cruisers and two destroyers. He then brought his F4F in to land. Queried about his earlier statements regarding two enemy carriers, the pilot maintained he had said nothing of carriers. An examination of his coding device revealed that the poorly designed mechanism substituted one type of ship for another. According to Lieutenant Forrest E. Biard, a *Hypo* code-breaker aboard Fletcher's flagship, the Admiral responded with anger and despair, screaming at Nielsen, "Young man, do you know what you have done? [...] You have just cost the United States two carriers!" (Toll, 2012, 340).

Conversely, the rest of the bridge crew, several of whom left their own accounts, failed to notice this outburst. Throughout Biard's account, Fletcher constantly looks "foolish," "stupider" than any other officer Biard has seen, or admits in ludicrous distress to being pathetically inadequate to his job. Given the fact that Fletcher and Biard engaged in an acrimonious dispute over codes immediately after the latter boarded the *Yorktown,* Biard's later account of Fletcher's reactions appears more as a venomous attempt at character assassination for personal reasons than a sober description of the admiral's actual behavior.

Either way, Fletcher thought about the situation briefly and then decided to allow the sortie to continue. After all, the faulty intelligence at his disposal placed the Japanese carriers somewhere to the north, and the American craft might also find some excellent targets of opportunity among the Port Moresby Invasion Force. General Douglas MacArthur, meanwhile, did his best to assist Task Force 17 by sending out B-17 bombers on scouting and search missions over the Coral Sea.

At 10:22 AM, almost simultaneous with the first attack on the *Neosho* far away in the south, one of the B-17 crews radioed a sighting of *Shoho* and a handful of escorts to MacArthur's HQ. The *Lexington* and *Yorktown* strike groups would have a target after all.

In the meantime, confusion grew among the Japanese admirals. Reports soon indicated that the American ships in the south consisted of an oiler and a destroyer, and Takagi decided to recall his attack force. However, it proved too late do so rapidly, as the strike leader already dispersed his aircraft to search the sea for a carrier. Japanese flying boats located and shadowed Task Force 17, but they botched their reports, making the American force seem further away than in reality. Other scouts reported Crace's detached Task Force 17.3 variously as a group of battleships or carriers, creating even more difficulties for the Japanese decision-makers.

The only Japanese officer who looked at the data and correctly analyzed the situation, Vice Admiral Goto Aritomo, commanded the Moresby Escort Force, including cruisers and the light aircraft carrier *Shoho*. He ordered the actual invasion force to turn back north until the battle ended. He then moved his cruisers to support the *Shoho*, but the gap between had grown too large for them to close up and provide anti-aircraft shelter to the small flattop.

Just three aircraft formed a combat air patrol over *Shoho* – the "Auspicious Phoenix" – when the American squadrons sighted the carrier and moved in for the kill. The first visual contact with the Japanese vessel consisted of slender threads of white against the deep blue of the ocean, the unmistakable wakes of large ships on the move. With the clear air in the northern Coral Sea, the USN pilots spotted the wakes at a range of 40 miles.

The American squadrons banked east and closed. Lieutenant Commander Weldon Hamilton soon made out the pale rectangle of a flight deck gleaming in the sun. Thumbing on his radio, he announced, "I see one flattop bastard." But despite being caught completely by surprise, Captain Izawa Ishinosuke immediately issued an order for an evasive turn, to which the crew responded crisply. The carrier drew a semicircle of foam on the sea as it came around to port, just as the first American aircraft streaked down from the sky.

Commander William Ault and Lieutenant Commander Robert Dixon led their respective sections of aircraft in bombing runs, but missed the carrier. Some of the bombs landed close enough to throw Japanese airplanes off the deck with their concussive force, and the SBDs' machine gunners raked the deck and the Japanese manning sponson-mounted anti-aircraft guns. Though the Japanese sent up a barrage of anti-aircraft fire, none of it hit. American doctrine emphasized marksmanship and often brought down many Japanese attackers, while the Japanese, training their men to use "spray and pray" barrage fire, enjoyed much less success with their carriers' anti-aircraft batteries throughout the war.

After Ault's and Dixon's runs, Weldon Hamilton brought his SBD-3 in for a bombing run, along with 14 other SBDs of Bombing Two. Hamilton achieved the first hit on the carrier, a devastating direct hit: "The Jap was exactly downwind as I nosed down, simplifying my problem tremendously. My bomb, which was the first 1,000 pounder to hit, struck in the middle of the flight deck's width, just abaft amidships. As I looked back the entire after-portion of the flight deck was ablaze and pouring forth heavy black smoke." (Toll, 2012, 342).

The explosion on the *Shoho*

Aboard the *Shoho,* the first hit reduced the deck to shambles. Akira Tendo, a reporter on the aircraft carrier, recounted that after the "breath" of the explosion rushed over the ship, an officer near him began shouting insults at the Americans while holding a hand to his cheek where a fragment had slashed it open. Another nearby sailor bled out and died from a severed arm, while a third tried to keep his station with enough of the flesh blown off his thigh to show the bone. Looking down, Akira saw blood soaking into his pants from a leg wound, but he felt too much shame at the worse injuries of the other men to seek medical aid.

The *Shoho* managed to launch three more fighters to reinforce its CAP, but this action represented too little, too late. The skilled *Yorktown* squadrons roared down, pummeling the burning ship with 1,000-lb bombs and torpedoes. Squadron leader William O. Burch landed another direct hit, and 11 more bombs punched into the shattered vessel after that. Seven torpedoes also ripped into the hull, bursting it open like wet cardboard.

The Americans circled back around the ruined carrier, this time snapping photographs with their K-35 cameras. As the men watched, most elated, a few sickened, the *Shoho*'s bow sank until the flight deck sliced into the water. The ship's propellers, still turning at full speed, helped drive the *Shoho* under the surface; the ship "ploughed herself under" according to Harold Buell, and the reporter Akira's account agrees. Out of the 834 men on board the *Shoho*, only 203, including Captain Izawa, survived to be rescued by *Sazanami*, an IJN destroyer. For their part, the Americans lost just three SBD Dauntless dive bombers in the attack. Built extremely tough like many American aircraft of World War II, the SBD-3s could often sustain multiple machine gun hits without crashing.

As the American airplanes streamed away from the spreading patch of reddish fuel oil on the clean blue Coral Sea's water, Lieutenant Commander Robert Dixon of the *Lexington* radioed an ecstatic message to Task Force 17: "Scratch one flattop! Dixon to Carrier, Scratch one flattop!" (Toll, 2012, 343).

When squadron commander Joseph Taylor landed on the *Yorktown,* he reported to the bridge with the other strike leaders, while his rear seat man hurried off to the ship's photo darkroom. When Taylor reached the bridge, Admiral Fletcher asked him what he had seen on the mission. Taylor responded that in a minute, he would show Fletcher. Fletcher at first believed Taylor sought to make him the butt of a joke, but in a short time, the rear seat man arrived with fully developed photographs of the *Shoho* burning and then sinking. The Admiral and the *Yorktown*'s captain forgot their dignity when they studied the still-dripping but conclusively detailed photos: "'When they looked at those pictures and heard the story,' said Joe, 'they jumped up and down like a couple of old grads in the grandstand when a last minute touchdown saves the day. Captain Buckmaster and Admiral Fletcher just threw their arms around Bill Burch and me and hugged us... they were so excited and happy.'" (Ludlum, 2006, 122).

The morning's error had paid off with the destruction of a light IJN carrier and all 21 attack aircraft on its deck. Better yet, the strike aircraft returned before any major Japanese raiding force arrived, despite the presence of skulking floatplanes for much of the day and the increasing crackle of Japanese radio traffic.

While the Americans celebrated their success, Crace's detached trio of cruisers and three destroyers came under air attack by Japanese land-based aircraft. The Australian and American ships maneuvered frantically, managing to avoid all the bombs dropped on them by the poorly trained land-based pilots. The latter returned to their bases with bombastic tales of victory, multiple "battleships" sunk, and the near-destruction of a major Allied surface fleet.

After the Japanese had flown off, a trio of American B-26 bombers spotted the Australian naval officer's command and, mistaking them for part of the Port Moresby Invasion Force, attacked. Crace later remarked, "Fortunately, their bombing, in comparison with that of the Japanese a few minutes earlier, was disgraceful." (Layton, 1985, 400).

To the south, the men aboard the fast oiler *Neosho,* skippered by Commander John Spinning Phillips, remained unaware of their peril until the wide formation of Japanese strike aircraft roared over the northern horizon at 10:28 AM. With skies rapidly clearing, the officers and sailors on *Neosho* and *Sims* clearly discerned the overwhelming force bearing down on them and scrambled to action stations despite the odds.

The first squadrons of Japanese aircraft dropped low and moved past the two American ships on a parallel course without immediately attacking. Though the USN personnel did not know it, these Japanese pilots radioed to their strike leader that a close visual inspection confirmed the *Neosho* was not an aircraft carrier. Accordingly, the strike leader sent most of the aircraft off in all directions in a search pattern, leaving 24 dive bombers and a handful of other aircraft to deal with the *Neosho*. These decisions made clear that the Japanese still assumed the scouting report had been correct and that an aircraft carrier had been present earlier, refueling from the fast oiler. Therefore, rather than returning to Vice Admiral Takagi's task force, the detached portion of the strike unit spent two hours combing the expanse of waters around the *Neosho*'s location, using up considerable fuel for no practical gains.

Grimly standing at their guns, the American crews raked the sky with a steady hail of anti-aircraft fire. The destroyer *Sims* fired flak shells from its 5 inch guns, while the *Neosho's* crew kept up a rapid barrage with their 20mm cannons and 40mm guns, as well as their 5-inch/38-caliber DP (dual-purpose) guns. The well-armed *Cimarron*-class fast oilers featured guns similar to those on American destroyers, though fewer in number (and the oilers also lacked the torpedoes found on all destroyers).

Three Nakajima B5N2 "Kate" torpedo bombers opened the attack, dropping a payload of bombs rather than Type 1 torpedoes. Under Phillips' coolheaded directions, the *Neosho* swerved hard to starboard, narrowly evading the bombs, which struck the sea surface in thunderous fountains of spray.

At this point Phillips ordered the *Neosho's* communications officer, Lieutenant William Driscoll, to radio the main task force with news of the situation. Driscoll, too terrified to function, merely radioed that three aircraft had bombed the *Neosho* and missed. Fletcher thus thought a small band of floatplanes had attacked the oiler and sent no fighters to its aid. Phillips later censured Driscoll sharply in his after-action report: "When contact with the enemy was made, the Commanding Officer directed this officer [...] to send out contact reports [...] The contact reports, and subsequent reports of this vessel's position when sinking, were not despatched correctly [...] His conduct under fire is questionable. [...] he should at least make an attempt to appear courageous even though inwardly frightened." (Phillips, 1942, 16).

The Japanese dive bombers took some time to set up their run. Finally, at one minute after noon, the Aichi D3A2 dive bombers stooped like falcons on their quarry. Dropping down the air in a long file, the Japanese pilots suddenly dispersed, their formation disintegrating as each man lined up to attack from a different direction.

The multidirectional attacks made both evasion and anti-aircraft fire more difficult. The *Sims* fired its five-inch guns as fast as the gunners could aim them. One shell struck a dive bomber full on, blasting the aircraft and its pilot into fragments that skimmed into the sea like buckshot, spattering the surface with small, foaming splashes.

However, at 12:15, the *Sims'* luck ran out. A Japanese bomb struck the aft deck, punching through into the engine room and exploding. Three more bombs hit the ship as it slid to a halt, no longer able to move or maneuver. Knowing an explosion would soon follow, the assistant chief engineer ordered the men nearby to put the whaleboats and life rafts in the water. The first whaleboat, damaged by bomb shrapnel, filled and sank immediately. A current pushed the second away from the ship,

Chief Signalman Robert Dicken and Fireman 2nd Class Vito J. Vessia, known to his shipmates as "Bill," swam to the drifting whaleboat, started its engine, and turned it back towards the *Sims*. The bomb hits had already thrown some men into the water, and Dicken witnessed the final moments of the sinking destroyer: "One outstanding act was done by an enlisted man named E.F. MUNCH, MM2c, just before he jumped over the side to be picked up by my boat, he secured a depth charge to the deck so it would not go over the side or accidentally explode on deck. The last I saw of the Commanding Officer he was standing on the bridge when the ship was blown up by the explosion. He showed an example of courage throughout the entire engagement." (Dicken, 1942, 3).

The *Sims*

When seawater flooded into the after engine room, the boilers exploded, followed almost immediately by a secondary explosion deep inside the hull. The central section of the *Sims* blew apart violently, splitting the destroyer in half. As the two halves abruptly sank, the forward five-inch gun crew fired a last defiant shot at the Japanese dive bombers, seconds before they vanished under the water.

Out of the crew of 192, only 15 survived to clamber aboard the whaleboat captained by Dicken and Vessia. Two of these men later died. The rest of the destroyer's crew, including skipper Lieutenant Commander Wilford Hyman, died in the explosions or drowned immediately afterward.

As the *Sims* met its demise, *Neosho* kept up a desperate fight against its tormenters. Bomb fragments sliced the head off one of the 20mm gunners and killed another, but the rest of the men stayed at their stations and continued firing. Two Japanese planes burst into flame and crashed into the ocean, while a third pilot, fatally hit, swerved his Aichi D3A2 into one of the 5-inch/38-caliber guns, inflicting tremendous damage on the fireroom just above the after engine room. The *Neosho* also took five direct hits from bombs, three near the bridge and two in the after section.

At 12:18 PM, the Japanese dive bombers ceased their attacks and flew away northward, believing the American oiler doomed. Phillips and his crew fought on doggedly to keep the ship afloat. With the ship afire and listing, steam blasting out of ruptured boilers, and wounded men screaming, some of the officers passed along the order to stand by to abandon ship. Many men only heard "abandon ship" in the confusion, however. They threw the inflatable life rafts over the side and leaped into the sea after them.

A picture of the burning ship

Nonetheless, Phillips managed to keep his ship afloat. He ordered the starboard wing tanks flooded to counteract a dangerous list to port which might have resulted in the oiler capsizing. The boilers lost steam without exploding, and the men brought the fires under control.

At this point, Phillips realized nearly two-thirds of the *Neosho's* 304-man crew had abandoned the ship prematurely. He sent out the whaleboats to tow them back, but the men in the boats found only a few of the rafts, whose gray color blended with the waves. 154 men and 4 officers disappeared into the vastness of the Coral Sea on tiny rafts.

The Japanese aircraft finally reached the relative safety of the *Zuikaku* and *Shokaku* after a 7-hour mission against one oiler and one destroyer. The men had no sooner climbed down from their cockpits, however, exhausted and ravenously hungry, than officers informed them that they would fly out on another strike as soon as a hasty refueling and rearming occurred. "King Kong"

Hara wanted to attack the actual American carriers without waiting for the morrow.

Obediently, Commander Takahashi Kakuishi, the strike leader, and his bone-weary aviators climbed back into their cockpits and took off into the failing evening light under heavy clouds. Part of the southern strike force still could not find the Japanese carriers, though radio traffic indicated their relatively close proximity. Takahashi accordingly led a reduced force against the two American carriers to the west.

The Japanese flew west, expecting a long flight to Task Force 17. In fact, the two armadas sailed quite close. The Americans' radar picked up the incoming attack formations and Fletcher ordered additional F4Fs scrambled, bulking up his combined carrier combat air patrol (CAP) to 30 Wildcats. As a result, Takahashi's attack group ran directly into an ambush set by F4Fs under two "hotshot" pilots, Lieutenant Commanders Paul Ramsey and James Flatley. The American pilots attacked the unsuspecting Japanese suddenly, accompanied by a radioed "Tally ho!" from Flatley. In short order, the Americans shot down eight Japanese aircraft, four of them accounted for by Ramsey alone.

Takahashi realized that if he lingered, the Wildcats would tear his whole force to ribbons. Accordingly, he ordered his surviving air crews to jettison their ordnance into the sea to lighten their loads, making them faster. Then he ordered his men to turn for the Japanese carriers and reach them as quickly as possible. As his strike force trailed away eastward, the *Lexington* and *Yorktown* began recovering their F4F fighters, working quickly due to the approach of dusk.

While the carriers recovered most of their aircraft by nightfall, they continued to cruise close to the same location in case any more stragglers arrived. Suddenly, at 7:09 PM, the men aboard the aircraft carriers observed large numbers of aircraft lights appear over the horizon. Most of the USN officers assumed that these numerous airplanes must belong to their other carrier's complement, since they had access to a count of only those aircraft that had returned to their own deck.

However, as the dark silhouettes of the aircraft flew closer, Lieutenant Commander Stroop on the *Lexington* spotted something amiss: "These planes were in very good formation. I remember noticing the port running lights of the formation all in a beautiful echelon, and one of the things that struck me as odd was that the red color of the port running light was different from the shade of running lights that we had on our own planes. They had a sort of a bluish tint, red-blue tint. About the time that we sighted these lights, one of our screen destroyers began firing at the planes." (Wooldridge, 1993, 39).

The sharp-eyed destroyer captain discerned that the silhouettes of the aircraft were those of Japanese, not American dive bombers. He therefore ordered his entire ship's anti-aircraft armament to open fire on the massed formations of Japanese craft. The flagship sent a desperate radio call to him to cease fire, to which the captain replied tartly that he knew Japanese airplanes when he saw them.

Incredibly, the Japanese aircraft were sending out identification queries and beginning to drop lower and slow as they prepared to land on the two American carriers, which they mistook for the *Zuikaku* and *Shokaku*. They suddenly found themselves in a sky blossoming with glaring bursts of flak and the brilliant stitched streamers of tracers. Abruptly, the Japanese pilots broke formation, swooping in all directions to baffle their opponents' aim as they streamed away across the sky.

The remaining F4F pilots eased back nervously to the *Lexington* and *Yorktown*, hoping that a nervous anti-aircraft gunner did not blow them out of the air. The Americans used radar to watch the Japanese aircraft retreat for approximately 40 miles before they faded from the display. This put the already battle-ready American crews even more on edge. While the relatively weak radar of the early World War II period could drop contacts at a range of several dozen miles or even less in sufficiently bad weather, the disappearing radar signatures could also mean the IJN carriers had moved extremely close.

The Japanese carriers, in fact, lay closer to their American counterparts than at any other moment in the battle, partially explaining the error of the Japanese pilots. A later estimate placed the two forces just 60 miles apart. The Americans listened in surprise to crystal-clear uncoded radio chatter between the carriers and the returning aircraft. Stroop once again furnished a vivid description: "One of the Japanese pilots couldn't get his wheels down, and the carrier told him [...] he'd have to land in the water. They wouldn't take him aboard, didn't want to clutter up their flight deck with a crash [...] So after he got this order from his air group commander or the captain of the Japanese carrier, he then requested that the carrier shine a light on the water so he'd have a spot to land on." (Wooldridge, 1993, 40).

As the interpreters provided rapid translations of the radio signals, the Americans heard the Japanese pilot repeat himself, this time angrily demanding that the ship switch on the spotlight. The chatter soon died down as the aircraft landed.

On the American side, the mistaken landing attempt by the Japanese cost two pilots their lives. 26-year-old Ensign John Drayton Baker, piloting an F4F Wildcat, attempted to land at the same time as the Japanese aircraft. Met by a spouting wall of anti-aircraft fire, Baker took his F4F away to the northeast to avoid the "friendly" batteries, and he soon lost his way amid the squalls. Unfortunately, a second Baker, Paul Baker, also flew his F4F through the darkness, but on the opposite side of the Task Force and in the opposite direction.

Admiral Fletcher took a personal interest in retrieving the unfortunate pilots. The fighter directors, Frank "Red" Gill of the *Lexington* and Oscar Pederson on the *Yorktown*, worked hard at their radios to bring the two desperate aviators in. Unfortunately, both pilots grew confused as to which directions they should be following; John Baker flew off northeast and Paul Baker flew off to the south to vanish forever.

John Baker, at around the same time Pederson attempted to give him directions to the nearest land, sent an ominous transmission hinting at his fate. He stated that he finally saw the *Yorktown* and began to circle it, yet the men on the *Yorktown* saw that his radar signature appeared dozens of miles away to the northeast, suggesting Baker had probably found a Japanese carrier and, like the Japanese earlier, mistook it for a "friendly." His final transmission at 8:28 PM stated, "Why don't you take me aboard? I'm almost out of fuel and am coming in to land." (Ludlum, 2006, 126).

While Paul Baker simply flew onward until his Wildcat likely nosed down into the remote expanse of the southern Coral Sea and he drowned, John Baker probably suffered a more violent end. Whether he crashed into the ocean, was thrown overboard after questioning by the Japanese, shot down, was killed later at a POW camp, or was slain accidentally when the Americans savaged the Japanese fleet carriers the following day, John Baker vanished without a trace.

Stuart D. Ludlum, a naval reservist, preserved the firsthand accounts of the two Bakers' deaths after conducting extensive interviews with the *Yorktown*'s aviators immediately after Midway. Later in the war, a "heroic myth" version of the story sprang up in which Paul Baker deliberately lured the Japanese aircraft wave away from the carrier group at the cost of his own splashdown and drowning.

Whatever the actual case, both Bakers received a posthumous Naval Cross. The USN named a *Cannon*-class destroyer escort, USS *Baker*, DE-190, after John Baker, while Paul Baker, who shot down three Japanese aircraft that day and damaged a fourth, had a *Buckley*-class destroyer escort, USS *Paul G. Baker*, DE-642, named after him.

To the east of Task Force 17, Admiral Takagi ordered his cruisers and destroyers to create a box of searchlight beams around his twin carriers. He knew the Americans' approximate location and thus felt safe in framing the two crucial vessels with light as a navigational aid to returning pilots. Presumably, the angry pilot asking for a spotlight on the sea surface also got his wish, enabling the retrieval of one more trained, experienced Japanese pilot from the water. By 9:30 PM, all surviving Japanese aircraft gathered back on the *Zuikaku* and *Shokaku*. Adnurak Takagi sailed east, while the Americans sailed southeast. This had the effect of slowly but steadily widening the gap between the hostile armadas. Morale on the Japanese ships suffered a severe blow upon learning of the *Shoho*'s destruction. Even the naval command experienced a wave of pessimism.

Around midnight, Fletcher and Fitch determined the American plan for the following day. Task Force 17 turned south, then due west, sailing further from the nearest Japanese land-based bomber bases. Fletcher intended to turn southeast at first light, whereupon Fitch would launch a full-circle search with *Lexington*'s scouts. The admiral set the search radius at 200 miles northward and 125 miles southward.

Chapter 6: May 8

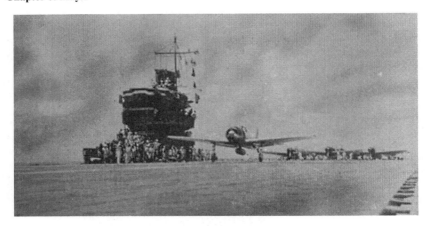

Planes taking off from the *Shokaku* on May 8

Brilliant tropical sunlight greeted Task Force 17 on the second day of the main Battle of the Coral Sea. The cold front had moved away to the north overnight, depriving the Americans of weather cover. The Japanese, however, still benefited from heavy squalls and cumulus towers, making the *Shokaku* and *Zuikaku* considerably less vulnerable.

Many of the men on board the two American aircraft carriers understood exactly how vulnerable the treacherously fair weather might prove, as noted by Signalman Floyd Beaver: "The next morning found us out in bright sunlight under clear skies with no place to hide. We got off our dawn searches and settled down to our usual waiting. But this time the wait was not so long as usual. Two of our search planes found the Japanese fast carriers, and we swung into the wind to launch our own attack [...] Unfortunately, the Japanese had found us as well and sent their airplanes winging against us." (Beaver, 2009, 166).

Many of the men, Fletcher included, got only three hours of sleep in the early morning of May 8th. Task Force 17 steamed west during the night, then turned southeast and used the trade winds to launch scouting aircraft and a strong CAP. At 8:20 AM, Lieutenant Joseph Smith spotted the Japanese carriers 175 miles away to the north of Task Force 17's position. Fletcher ordered the launch of two strike groups, then turned over tactical command of both carriers' complements to Fitch. The *Yorktown* put 15 SBD-3 dive bombers, 12 TBD-1 Devastator torpedo planes, and 9 F4F Wildcats into the air, while the *Lexington* launched 24 SBDs, 9 TBDs, and 6 F4Fs.

At around 9 AM, Dixon, who had announced "scratch one flattop" the day before, found the Japanese fleet and gave a more accurate location and distance, 191 miles from Task Force 17. The intrepid pilot shadowed the Japanese for an hour, slipping between storms to escape the Zero fighters that soon began hunting him, all the while transmitting valuable data to Fitch.

The Japanese immediately changed course and launched 69 aircraft against Fletcher's armada – 18 torpedo bombers, 33 carrier bombers, and 18 fighters. Once again, Commander Takahashi served as the strike leader. Once all the aircraft left the carriers' decks, Hara ordered the two vessels and their escorts up to a speed of 30 knots, making directly for the American battlegroup. This eased his retrieval of his own aircraft but also brought the *Zuikaku* and *Shokaku* deeper into the USN aerial strike force's attack zone.

One of the Japanese scouts, Kanno Kenzo, located Task Force 17 at 8:22 AM and gave "King Kong" Hara surprisingly accurate location, heading, and distance information. The USN CAP pilots never spotted the wily Kanno, who switched on his homing signal as he flitted ghostlike around the task force's periphery, guiding the Japanese strike planes directly to his location. The F4F Wildcats flushed out a land-based flying boat, however, and destroyed it.

Fletcher deployed Task Force 17 in an anti-aircraft circle, with the carriers in the center about two miles apart, a ring of destroyers around them, and the cruisers in an outer ring. While the Japanese expressed scorn for this formation, apparently relying purely on anti-aircraft firepower, Fletcher actually expected maneuvering by the carriers to form an important part of the defense.

The American strikes reached the Japanese carriers slightly before the Japanese attack reached their targets, at 10:32 AM. However, William Burch, the strike leader for the *Yorktown's* aircraft, opened the action with a serious mistake. Both *Zuikaku* and *Shokaku* sailed in the open when he and his dive bombers arrived on the scene, but Burch delayed, waiting for the slower TBD-1 torpedo bombers to catch up. During this time, *Zuikaku* slid neatly into a heavy squall and vanished from sight.

When the torpedo bombers finally arrived at around 10:52 AM, both sets of aircraft launched attacks against the *Shokaku,* the only remaining target. The Japanese aircraft carrier swerved and turned to avoid the bombs and torpedoes, while Zero fighters darted out to harass the American aircraft, shooting some down, damaging others, and spoiling the attack runs of yet others.

The first squadron, that of Burch, scored no hits at all on the *Shokaku.* As the Americans dove from the cold air aloft to the warm, humid air closer to sea level, their canopies and telescopic sights fogged over in precisely the same manner as at Tulagi. In the meantime, the TBD-1s, unable to approach the Japanese carriers due to their fighter cover, launched their torpedoes vainly from extreme range.

The second attack, led by Lieutenant Walter Short, involved 17 SBD-3s. Once again, the pale obscurity of fogging blinded the pilots as their dive bombers streaked downward across the sky. Nevertheless, Lieutenant John Powers dove lower than the rest, determined to score a hit no matter what the cost. Having told others pilots in the attack force that he would "get a direct hit if I have to lay it on the flight deck," Powers plunged to 900 feet altitude and released his bomb. The stout, capsule-shaped piece of ordnance hurtled across the gap and plunged into the *Shokaku's* deck, followed by a shattering explosion just aft of the Japanese carrier's bridge. Touching off aviation fuel, the blast started a ferocious blaze, whose glare the other pilots compared to an acetylene torch.

Powers paid heavily for his courage. Possibly damaged by the blast of his own bomb, his SBD-3 flashed downwards towards the sea to the starboard of the *Shokaku*. Powers tried to pull up at 200 feet, but the Dauntless dive bomber smashed into the sea surface, killing both Powers (who received a posthumous Medal of Honor) and his copilot. A second SBD-3 scored a hit during this attack.

Powers

The Japanese made excellent use of the weather cover provided by the "quasi-stationary" cold front, which now covered them rather than the American carriers. Lieutenant Noel Gayler described the conditions prevailing during the action: "You couldn't see much [...] Big towering columns of rain clouds, sort of like pillars. You'd go around them and all of a sudden you'd see the carrier. Here he is, and there he's gone [...] It was just such an incredibly confusing, mixed-up, screwed up situation. Poor visibility and people yelling on the radio." (Toll, 2012, 354).

The American aircraft lost track of *Shokaku* after Powers' attack, despite the extensive fires burning on the deck and the huge cloud of black smoke trailing from the wounded carrier. Slightly later, William Ault of the *Lexington* and three other SBD pilots found the *Shokaku* once more, using a "box" search pattern.

A picture of the *Shokaku* under attack

A picture of the *Shokaku*'s crew fighting fires on deck

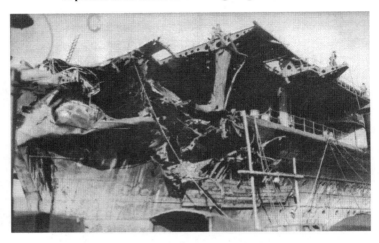

A picture of damage to the bow

The quartet of aircraft immediately attacked, scoring another hit on the carrier – the third and last of the day. Though the TBDs launched many torpedoes against the *Shokaku,* all either missed or struck the hull and failed to detonate, both characteristic flaws of the inferior quality of the torpedoes used by the U.S. Navy in the early war years.

Meanwhile, two American ensigns flying TBD-1 Devastator torpedo bombers located the *Zuikaku* and tried to attack. Thomas Bash and Norman Sterrie released their torpedoes regardless of the Zeros trying to shoot them down, but only at extreme range. Neither torpedo came close to hitting its target, and the Americans lost two SBD-3s and three F4F Wildcats to the Zero CAP during the action, while many others suffered damage.

As this took place, the Japanese strike located the American carriers, utterly exposed on the sunlit ocean. Kanno Kenzo, the scout who successfully shadowed Task Force 17 for over an hour without being seen, matched courses with strike leader Takahashi. With consummate professionalism and samurai fatalism, Kanno guided the Japanese squadrons over the last few miles to their objective, ensuring the attack reached its target in the fastest time possible. This represented a death sentence for Kanno and his two crew, who exhausted their fuel during the shadowing and guiding.

As his radar screen suddenly lit up with 69 incoming "bogeys," the *Lexington*'s fighter controller, "Red" Gill, shouted into the radio the decades-old rallying call of carnival personnel at the start of an all-out fight: "Hey, Rube!" The Americans had 17 F4F Wildcats airborne, along with a supplemental force of SBD-3 Dauntlesses Fitch wanted to use in an air-to-air role.

Unfortunately, the order went out to fly low to guard against torpedo bombers, enabling the Japanese to pass over some of the American CAP. The Japanese aircraft brushed past the outer CAP and went into the attack runs. A furious melee between the combat air patrol and the escorting Zeros broke out, while the dive bombers and torpedo bombers sought their targets. Most of the aircraft to be used against *Yorktown* had been shot down in the dusk ambush the night before, so the preponderance of the attacking force made their runs at the *Lexington*.

The leader of the Type 97 torpedo bombers, Lieutenant Commander Shimazaki Shigekazu, left a vivid account of the scene as he brought his aircraft in for an attack on the *Lexington*, which he nearly accidentally rammed as he pulled out of his attack run: "Never in all my years in combat have I even imagined a battle like that! When we attacked the enemy carriers, we ran into a virtual wall of antiaircraft fire; the carriers and their supporting ships blackened the sky with exploding shells and tracers. It seemed impossible that we could survive our bombing and torpedo runs through such incredible defenses. [...] Burning and shattered planes of both sides plunged from the skies. Amidst this fantastic 'rainfall' of antiaircraft and spinning planes, I dove almost to the water's surface and sent my torpedo into the *Saratoga*-type carrier." (Okumiya, 1956, 103).

The Type 99 dive bombers also screamed in to drop bombs on the *Lexington* as smaller numbers of each type attacked the *Yorktown*. The *Lexington*, huge and unwieldy, tried to turn out of the way of the attacks, but too slowly to avoid some of them. The *Yorktown*, on the other hand, showed itself much more nimble, moving rapidly out of the way of torpedoes and even dodging bombing runs with abrupt zigzags. Only a single bomb struck the *Yorktown*, inflicting relatively minor damage and a quickly extinguished fire, and at some point during the melee, the strike leader, Lieutenant Commander Takahashi Kakuichi, suffered a hit from either the innumerable flak bursts or an F4F Wildcat. His plane plunged burning into the sea, killing him.

While the *Yorktown* avoided serious damage, the *Lexington* lacked the good fortune of its lighter cousin. Captain Sherman, calm despite the "majestic" slowness of his vessel, tried to turn his ship out of the way of the Japanese torpedoes streaking the water in every direction. The torpedoes porpoised, leaping out of the water and then plunging back in as their powerful motors drove them forward. This gave Stanley Johnston, aboard the *Lexington*, the eerie feeling of the ordnance as living creatures hunting his ship: "Their wicked noses look to me like death incarnate. I have the illusion they are alive, and breaking water to peek at us, only to dive again after having made sure of their courses." (Johnston, 1942, 184).

The huge aircraft carrier, skillfully handled, managed to avoid damage for several minutes. At one point, Sherman kept the vessels on a straight course to allow a pair of torpedoes to pass it by, one running parallel to the hull on either side. But eventually, the large number of attackers and the ship's own ponderousness caused its luck to run out. Two bombs exploded on board the *Lexington*, and two torpedoes struck home in its hull, ripping away armored plate. The explosions killed dozens of men with shrapnel or flame that instantly baked them into carbonized lumps, and they started raging fires.

After a desperate fight with firefighting foam, the Americans managed to put out the flames and began taking the F4Fs aboard. Unfortunately, the ship's doom gathered below decks even as the men began to relax. Thick gasoline fumes from leaking tanks filled the air, growing ever more concentrated until the sparks from a damaged power cable near the telephone switchboard touched them off. The colossal blast wrenched the vessel from the keel up and sent a flaming blast through the ship, instantly killing 25 men and injuring dozens more.

Lieutenant H.E. Williamson later recalled in an interview: "Immediately following the explosion, a gale of wind with the force of a hurricane blew through the door from Central and pinned me to the board. The wind seemed to be made up of streams of flame and myriads of sparks [...] and left nothing but heavy choking fumes. [...] There were cries from the surrounding rooms, so I shouted at the top of my voice, 'Take it easy and hold your breath, and we'll all get out.'" (Johnston, 1942, 244).

The first blast occurred at 12:47 PM, and at first, the captain and crew did not realize the fatal situation of the carrier. However, the explosion ripped open doors and bulkheads, enabling the volatile fumes to spread throughout the ship's interior. Firefighters continued struggling with the flames for hours, but dozens of small explosions occurred, each adding to the inferno and spreading it to new areas.

Pictures of the *Lexington* on fire

At 2:42 PM, a huge explosion destroyed the forward elevator. Another shattering blast rocked the ship at 3:25 PM, after which both Sherman and Fitch realized the necessity of abandoning the *Lexington*. At 4 PM, the captain ordered the engines shut down and the remaining steam vented to prevent a boiler explosion. The men then began a massive rescue operation, combing the burning decks below for wounded or trapped men. The heroic efforts of the crew, who showed great courage and steadiness in the face of the perilous situation, saved hundreds of men who would otherwise have perished in the depths of the vessel.

At 5:07 PM, Admiral Fitch issued the order to abandon ship, seemingly tired of waiting for Sherman to issue the command. The crew did so without panic or haste in a remarkably orderly fashion. Harold Littlefield noted the calm atmosphere aboard the "Lady Lex" during its final moments, despite the possibility of a massive explosion: "Those who were back aft had a treat that we on the bow missed out on. The ice cream locker was aft on the main deck so they broke her open and all the fellows there had all the ice cream they could eat. [...] The morale of the men was excellent; I don't remember seeing any signs of panic. In fact, shortly before leaving ship I saw one fellow lying on the flight deck reading a magazine!" (Hoehling, 1971, 171).

Last to leave the ship at around 6 PM were the executive officer, Mort Seligman, and Captain Sherman himself. Sherman lingered for a moment until a huge explosion erupted through the deck, filling the air with broken airplanes. Seligman shouted for him to follow, and as the two men slid down the rope into the water, Sherman remarked, "I was just thinking, wouldn't I look silly if I left this ship and the fires went out?" (Toll, 2012, 366). In fact, Sherman left just in time.

30 minutes later, a vast explosion went up into the night sky as the *Lexington* blew apart from the inside. Debris and aircraft rained down on the sea for hundreds of yards around as the *Lexington* turned into a pyre of dark red flames. The destroyers and cruisers moved in to rescue the crew, with the USS *Minneapolis* saving Sherman from the water. With the survivors safely aboard, Fletcher sent the USS *Phelps* in to sink the hulk with torpedoes. Shortly after the colossal wreck slid under the waters, a huge explosion occurred, its shock felt and heard by ships 10 miles distant. Out of 2,951 men on board the *Lexington*, 216 died, and 36 aircraft on the carrier's deck sank into the sea.

Chapter 7: The Results

Fletcher, knowing the loss of the *Yorktown* could turn the situation into a complete disaster, ordered a retreat. Task Force 17 sailed south, then east, slipping out of the Coral Sea to refuel at Tonga. Task Force 17.3 under Crace, nearly out of fuel, sailed for the Australian ports, while the fast oiler *Neosho*'s crew, working tirelessly, managed to keep the ship afloat for four days despite its gaping wounds and shattered boilers. The whaleboat captained by Dicken and Vessia came alongside, taking on containers of food and water from the larger ship. The oiler and the whaleboat remained together during the four-day wait for rescue. Finally, the destroyer USS *Henley* arrived on May 11th and took the survivors of both the *Neosho* and *Sims* aboard. The *Henley* then used its torpedoes to sink the tattered oiler and the whaleboat lashed to its side.

The USS *Helm,* another destroyer, found one of the *Neosho's* life rafts drifting five days later, on May 16th, 1942. The *Helm* picked up four survivors from the raft, of whom one died soon after rescue. The three survivors reported that they originally numbered 68, crowded onto four life rafts lashed together. However, 64 of the men died from thirst while awaiting rescue. The *Helm* took the three to Brisbane for medical treatment, where another man died. Thus, only two of the 158 officers and men who abandoned the *Neosho* survived.

In light of these facts, Phillips made a list of four recommendations as part of his report. The first addressed the problem of finding life rafts: "That all life rafts be painted yellow, and provided with a tarpaulin which can be quickly slipped off; tarpaulin to be painted the color of the surrounding structure. The Neosho life rafts were painted grey and were extremely difficult for the men in the water, and personnel on board ship, or for searching ships or aircraft, to locate in the water." (Phillips, 1942, 16). While no direct link exists, the USN soon adopted chrome yellow life rafts, which remained in use until replaced by even more visible red life rafts in 1952. The *Neosho's* experience in the Coral Sea may well have helped prompt the change to colorful rafts.

The Japanese also retreated. Inoue requested permission to retreat from Admiral Yamamoto, the architect of the attack on Pearl Harbor, who initially angrily refused. With no forces left opposing them, the Japanese could have readily taken Port Moresby, but they declined to do so. Though *Shokaku* required repairs and could not support air operations from its mangled deck, *Zuikaku* remained and the invasion force also remained intact. Okumiya Masatake later blasted his commanders in a postwar book for abandoning the opportunity of a notable strategic success and a continued Japanese advance: "The truth of the matter was that our senior naval commanders in the Coral Sea area lacked the fighting spirit necessary to engage the enemy. This failure to pursue a temporary advantage later proved to be of tremendous advantage to the Americans (Okumiya, 1956, 110). As at the Battle of Leyte Gulf, Japanese commanders proved remarkably fragile once the enemy pierced their feelings of invincibility, "giving up" too soon and squandering the opportunities won for them by the courage and blood of their subordinates.

The fame of engagements such as the Battle of Midway overshadows the Battle of the Coral Sea in historic memory, but Coral Sea proved quite significant to the course of World War II in the Pacific. Though the Japanese claimed a victory after sinking the USS *Lexington,* the battle actually gave the Imperial Japanese Navy its first bloody nose in a conflict which, until then, had been going entirely their way. This dented Japanese morale and raised that of the Americans, Australians, and British, beginning a tidal shift in the balance of confidence which previously favored the warriors of Japan over the Allies. Rather than being in "high spirits for an adventure" as had been the case just a few days before, Inoue's official diary revealed a new, anxious, almost pessimistic outlook: "The dream of a great victory is gone. The battle belongs to the enemy. It was impossible, as feared. When the expected enemy raid came, we could not even mobilise the slightest united strength. In the end, we cannot even blame inadequate reconnaissance seaplanes. I am all the more concerned." (Bullard, 2007, 63).

While the outcome of the tactical engagement represented something of a draw, or a result slightly in the favor of the Japanese, the Americans clearly won on the strategic level. The Japanese carriers withdrew, and in doing so they aborted the seaborne invasion of Port Moresby. A land attack on the key port also failed thanks to the hard-fighting Australians. The base never fell to the Japanese and became an important center in the counteroffensive that eventually crushed the Empire of Japan in the coming years.

More immediately, the Battle of the Coral Sea helped the Americans achieve their notable victory at the Battle of Midway in several ways. The sinking of *Shoho* prevented the light carrier's possible deployment at the June naval encounter, and *Shokaku* suffered too much damage to participate in the later fight. *Zuikaku*, though still in fighting condition, lost most of its aircraft complement in the battle off Australia, and therefore the Japanese did not deploy it at Midway either. As a result, the outcome of the May 7th to 8th naval encounter reduced the number of Japanese carriers at Midway by at least two vessels, and possibly three.

The Battle of the Coral Sea likewise firmly established the reputation of Joseph Rochefort as a master codebreaker, known to the highest levels of the USN hierarchy, including Admirals Chester Nimitz and Ernest King. These men therefore gave considerable weight to his pronouncements about Midway as the next Japanese objective, based on his unique analysis of signals intelligence, when planning their countermeasures against Yamamoto Isoroku's next move. As Rochefort later stated, "We were a little surprised that [King] would ask us what our views were. I personally felt that he was not even aware of our existence." (Carson, 2011, 282).

The Coral Sea operation provided a superb "proof of concept" for Joe Rochefort's skills and the methods of the whole *Hypo* code-breaking team. Therefore, when he later made one of his penetrating leaps of intuition that a mysterious objective labeled "AF" corresponded to Midway Island, and he telephoned Lieutenant Commander Edwin Layton, Nimitz's intelligence chief, to announce, "I've got something so hot here it's burning the top of my desk," Layton worked to convince Nimitz of the code-breaker's accuracy. The Admiral, knowing Rochefort's earlier work, soon agreed.

Thus it transpired that Yamamoto arrived at Midway with four rather than seven carriers in his armada, and, rather than a weakly defended island, he found a powerful American carrier force awaiting him. In the ensuing battle, Yamamoto lost all four of his irreplaceable heavy carriers, crippling the IJN's offensive capability and permanently changing the course of the war in the Pacific theater. Both conditions contributing to his defeat – the reduced carrier force at his disposal and the presence of the American fleet – sprang from events that unfolded exactly one month before during the somewhat forgotten but pivotal Battle of the Coral Sea, the first naval battle in history to be fought entirely by carrier sorties rather than gunfire.

The era of the aircraft carrier had fully arrived.

Online Resources

Other World War II titles by Charles River Editors

Other titles about Coral Sea on Amazon

Bibliography

Beaver, Floyd. *Sailor from Oklahoma: One Man's Two-Ocean War.* Annapolis, 2009.

Bullard, Steven (translator). *Japanese Army Operations in the South Pacific Area: New Britain and Papua Campaigns, 1942-1943.* Canberra, 2007.

Carson, Elliot. *Joe Rochefort's War: The Odyssey of the Codebreaker Who Outwitted*

Yamamoto at Midway. Annapolis, 2011.

Dicken, Robert James, CSM. *Personal observations of SIMS #409 disaster.* Action report; https://www.ibiblio.org/hyperwar/USN/ships/logs/DD/dd409-Coral.html; retrieved June 24th, 2016; original report May 18th, 1942.

Hoehling, A.A. *The Lexington Goes Down: The Last Seven Hours of a Fighting Lady.* Englewood Cliffs, 1971.

Hoyt, Edwin P. *Blue Skies and Blood: The Battle of the Coral Sea.* New York, 2003.

Johnston, Stanley. *Queen of the Flat Tops: The USS Lexington and the Coral Sea Battle.* New York, 1942.

Layton, Edwin T. *And I Was There: Pearl Harbor and Midway – Breaking the Secrets.* New York, 1985.

Ludlum, Stuart D. *They Turned the War Around at Coral Sea and Midway: Going to War With Yorktown's Air Group Five.* Bennington, 2006.

Lundstrom, John B. *Black Shoe Carrier Admiral: Frank Jack Fletcher at Coral Sea, Midway, and Guadalcanal.* Annapolis, 2006.

Okumiya, Masatake, Horikoshi Jiro, and Martin Caidin. *Zero!* New York, 1956.

Phillips, John S. *Engagement of U.S.S. NEOSHO with Japanese Aircraft on May 7, 1942; Subsequent Loss of U.S.S. NEOSHO; Search for Survivors.* Action report; https://www.ibiblio.org/hyperwar/USN/ships/logs/AO/ao23-Coral.html; retrieved June 24th, 2016; original report May 25th, 1942.

Stille, Mark. *The Coral Sea 1942: The First Carrier Battle.* Botley, 2009.

Toll, Ian W. *Pacific Crucible: War at Sea in the Pacific, 1941-1942.* New York, 2012.

Wooldridge, E.T. *Carrier Warfare in the Pacific: An Oral History Collection.* Washington DC, 1993.

Made in the USA
Monee, IL
13 September 2020

42416384R00031